North American
# INDIAN NATIONS

---

# NATIVE PEOPLES
## of the
# SOUTHEAST

Linda Lowery

LERNER PUBLICATIONS ◆ MINNEAPOLIS

Consultant: Karenne Wood (Monacan), Director of the Virginia Indian Programs at the Virginia Foundation for the Humanities in Charlottesville, Virginia

Lerner Publications Company
A division of Lerner Publishing Group, Inc.
241 First Avenue North
Minneapolis, MN 55401 USA

For reading levels and more information, look up this title at www.lernerbooks.com.

Main body text set in Rockwell Std Light 12/16.
Typeface provided by Monotype Typography.

**Library of Congress Cataloging-in-Publication Data**

Lowery, Linda.
    Native peoples of the Southeast / Linda Lowery.
        pages cm. — (North American Indian nations)
    Includes bibliographical references.
    ISBN 978-1-4677-7935-7 (lb : alk. paper) — ISBN 978-1-4677-8327-9 (pb : alk. paper) — ISBN 978-1-4677-8328-6 (eb pdf)
    1. Indians of North America—Southern States—History—Juvenile literature. 2. Indians of North America—Southern States—Social life and customs—Juvenile literature. I. Title.
E78.S65L69 2016
975.004'97—dc23                                                    2015012385

Manufactured in the United States of America
1 – PC – 7/15/16

# CONTENTS

INTRODUCTION 5

CHAPTER 1
LIVING WITH THE LAND 10

CHAPTER 2
COMMUNITY AND SPIRITUALITY 18

CHAPTER 3
ART, MUSIC, AND DANCE 24

CHAPTER 4
PEACETIME AND WARTIME 30

CHAPTER 5
BLENDING PAST AND FUTURE 38

NOTABLE SOUTHEAST INDIANS 42
TIMELINE 43
GLOSSARY 44
SOURCE NOTES 45
SELECTED BIBLIOGRAPHY 45
FURTHER INFORMATION 46
INDEX 47

ARCTIC

SUBARCTIC

NORTHWEST COAST

PLATEAU

GREAT BASIN

PLAINS

NORTHEAST

CALIFORNIA

SOUTHWEST

SOUTHEAST

# SOUTHEAST
## REGION OF NORTH AMERICA

### CULTURAL REGIONS OF THE UNITED STATES AND CANADA

| | | |
|---|---|---|
| Plateau | Southeast | Subarctic |
| Northwest Coast | Southwest | Arctic |
| California | Great Basin | Other |
| Plains | Northeast | |

- - - Cultural area border

——— International border

········· State/province border

# INTRODUCTION

**T**he elders gathered their people for a council. They decided to travel in search of a new homeland. The creator of all things had given the people a special gift. It was a sacred pole to guide the way. It was called the *kohta falaya*, or the long pole. Every night, the people planted the pole in the ground, pointing it straight up to the sky. By morning, the pole leaned east, toward the rising sun.

The people followed the direction of the sacred pole. They were led by the chief of the Chickasaw (CHICK-uh-saw) and the chief of the Choctaw (CHOK-taw). They crossed grasslands and hills and a great river, wider than they had ever seen. They walked for days, months, and years. One night, they camped at a place called Nanih Waiya. The next morning, the pole still stood perfectly straight. The people knew they were home.

## A Long History

**The Chickasaw and the Choctaw tell this sacred story of how they came to live in the southeastern United States.** The Southeast has been home to many American Indian peoples for at least fifteen thousand years. Some of these

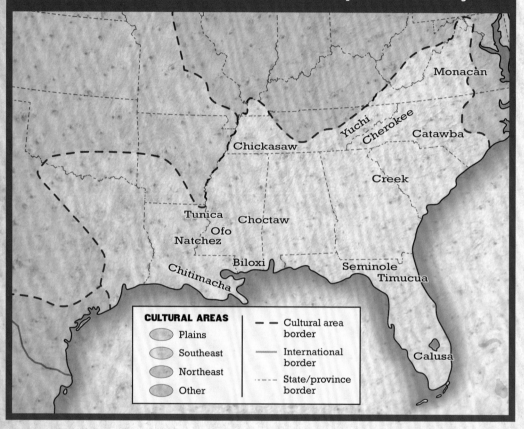

# PEOPLES OF THE SOUTHEAST

The Southeast region was the original home of many American Indian nations. This map shows the areas where some of them lived before Europeans arrived in the region.

Monacàn

Yuchi
Cherokee
Catawba

Chickasaw

Creek

Tunica
Ofo
Choctaw
Natchez

Biloxi
Seminole
Timucua

Chitimacha

**CULTURAL AREAS**

Plains

Southeast

Northeast

Other

– – Cultural area
      border

—— International
      border

-·-·- State/province
      border

Calusa

people may have come from the north. Others may have come to the Southeast from Mexico and Cuba.

Peoples such as The Mississippians, or Mound Builders, built temples of huge mounds of earth as early as 800 CE. The biggest Mound Builder city, called Cahokia, was built on the Mississippi River in present-day Illinois. The city's largest mound

The Nanih Waiya Mound in Mississippi is 140 feet (43 m) wide.

covered 16 acres (6.5 hectares) and stood 100 feet (31 meters) high. The remains of Mound Builder settlements have been found in Mississippi, Louisiana, Georgia, Arkansas, and Florida. The Choctaw, Natchez (NATCH-is), and other groups probably descended from the Mound Builders. The Creek, who call themselves Muskogee (muss-KOH-ghee), are a union of several peoples who also descended from the Mound Builders. This union is sometimes called the Creek Confederacy.

## Language Families
**Historically, the Southeast Indians spoke languages from four language families.** Some groups spoke languages called isolates, which are unlike any other in the world. The Calusa (cuh-LOO-suh), Tequesta (tuh-KESS-tuh), and Tunica (TYOON-uh-cuh) spoke isolate languages.

# LANGUAGE FAMILIES OF THE SOUTHEAST PEOPLES

| LANGUAGE FAMILY | PEOPLES |
|---|---|
| Muskogean | Choctaw, Chickasaw, Creek, and Seminole |
| Iroquoian | Cherokee |
| Siouan | Catawba, Ofo, Biloxi, Yuchi, Santee, Monacan, and others |
| Caddoan | Caddo |

Traditionally, peoples that belonged to the same language family lived near one another.

The Creek spoke a Muskogean language. People who spoke this language lived across the Southeast. Their land was dotted with hickory trees, which they used for firewood. They used the nuts for oil, and for making nut milk and soup. The Choctaw, Chickasaw, and Natchez settled in present-day Mississippi and Louisiana.

The Cherokee (CHAIR-uh-key) were the only Iroquoian-speaking people of the Southeast. They settled about two thousand years ago in the Appalachian Mountains of present-day Tennessee, North Carolina, South Carolina, and Georgia.

Peoples who spoke Siouan languages included the Catawba (keh-TAW-beh), Biloxi (buh-LOX-ee), Yuchi (YOO-chee), Monacan (MON-uh-kin), Ofo (oh-foh), and Santee (san-TEE). The Catawba settled along the river valleys in modern-day North and

South Carolina. They gathered herbs, berries, and nuts. They ate fish from the rivers and deer and elk from the forests.

The only Southeast members of the Caddoan language family were the Caddo (CAD-oh). The Caddo settled along rivers in present-day Louisiana, Texas, and Arkansas. They traveled by river in dugout canoes carved from the cypress trees on their land.

## European Arrival

**In the mid-sixteenth century, Europeans began to arrive in the region.** The lives of the Southeast Indians changed forever. Europeans wanted to live on land that was sacred to the Southeast Indians. The Europeans also brought diseases the Southeast Indians could not fight. In the 1830s, the US government forced most Southeast Indians to move west. But Southeast peoples remain tied to their homelands, their languages, and the traditions that were shaped by the land.

# CHAPTER 1

# LIVING WITH THE LAND

**T**he Southeast is a land of mountains, river valleys, jungles, swamps, and waterfalls. The area is bordered by the Atlantic Ocean to the east and the Gulf of Mexico to the south. The northern part of the region, near the Appalachian Mountains, is hilly and forested. The western part of the region extends to the grasslands of the Great Plains.

Saltwater marshes cover much of the land at the coast, where the Santee settled. The climate is hot and humid to the south, where the Biloxi and Natchez lived along southern rivers. The Calusa and later the Seminole (SEM-in-ole) settled in the humid jungles and wet grasslands of the Everglades in modern-day Florida. The Cherokee were surrounded by the Appalachian Mountains with its waterfalls, cool yellow pine forests, and winter snow.

The land gave the people everything they needed for shelter, food, and clothing. For many generations, Southeast Indians moved from place to place, hunting animals for food. Around 800 CE, corn arrived in the area through trade with other nations. After that, most Southeast Indians farmed more than they hunted.

This photo of a Seminole mother and her children was taken around 1915.

Some Southeast peoples built short-term settlements when they traveled. They built villages near water, on land with rich soil. They changed the landscape by burning some forests to add space for orchards, fields, and farms.

## Homes

Some Southeast Indians lived in cities with thousands of people. Others lived in smaller communities. The Cherokee settled in villages along rivers in the Great Smoky Mountains. Their villages ranged from fifty people to six hundred people. The Timucua (tim-uh-KOO-uh) lived in about 150 villages across what is now northern Florida. They were a powerful nation of fifty thousand to two hundred thousand people. The Creek spread out across the Southeast. They built towns along rivers from the Appalachian Mountains to the Atlantic coast. The Chickasaw lived in small camps scattered along waterways.

Many towns were surrounded by palisades. These fences were made of tall, sturdy poles stuck into the ground. They protected the town from attacks by other nations. They also kept out wild animals. Some villages had a central area with a large building in the middle. People gathered there for ceremonial dances and councils. The

This early drawing shows a Southeast Indian village protected by palisades.

Cherokee built large, seven-sided council buildings in their village centers.

Southeast Indians used materials that were common where they lived. The most common style of home was wattle and daub. These homes were built by covering woven twigs and grasses with mud. The mud hardened in the heat of the sun, making the homes sturdy. The Creek and Cherokee lived in wattle-and-daub homes.

The Cherokee used a strong grass called river cane to make mats to cover the ceilings of their wattle-and-daub homes. They also used river cane to make furniture. The posts for their homes

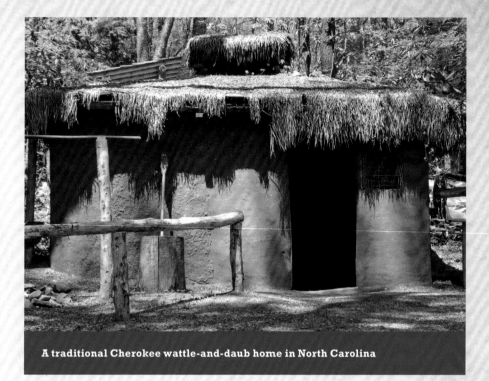

A traditional Cherokee wattle-and-daub home in North Carolina

were usually made of dried wood. The Monacan covered their cone-shaped homes with shingles of tree bark from the forests around them.

The Seminole lived in houses called chickees made from palmetto trees. They had thatched roofs of grass or palmetto leaves. The houses were built on stilts high off the ground to protect against snakes, other animals, and flooding. There was a platform inside for sleeping and another higher platform for storage.

Some groups, such as the Chickasaw, had seasonal houses. In summer they lived in homes with open sides to keep cool. In winter they moved to wattle-and-daub homes that were dug into the ground for protection from the cold.

## Food

The Southeast offered plenty of wild animals to hunt. The Southeast peoples hunted deer, black bear, elk, otters, and raccoons. People also hunted turkeys, ducks, and other birds. They got fish and oysters from the rivers and ocean. In the areas that became Florida and Louisiana, the Natchez, Biloxi, and Seminole ate turtles and alligators.

The land also had plenty of berries, fruits, and nuts. The Cherokee gathered crabapples, grapes, and nuts from the

# HUNTING AND GATHERING

| PEOPLES | WILD FOODS |
|---------|------------|
| Caddo | Buffalo, deer, turkey, rabbit, fish, salt, and sunflower seeds |
| Cherokee | Deer, turtles, buffalo, bear, cattails, mushrooms, chestnuts, walnuts, butternuts, plums, crabapples, and grapes |
| Natchez | Deer, turkey, bear, buffalo, duck, fish, clams, oysters, crayfish, wild rice, pecans, berries, grapes, mushrooms, and persimmons |
| Seminole | Otter, raccoon, bobcat, turtle, alligator, birds, deer, wild boar, pineapples, mangoes, guava, oranges, and mulberries |
| Tequesta | Shark, sailfish, porpoise, turtle eggs, lobster, manatee, wild boar, sea grapes, palmetto berries, and palm nuts |

meadows and the woods. The Tequesta ate wild palmetto berries, sea grapes, and palm nuts. The Creek collected wild potatoes.

The Southeast was a rich region for farming. There was fruitful soil and strong sunshine. Rivers, rain, and springs gave plenty of water. Families cleared areas to grow food for their household. They also shared fields to grow crops.

The Cherokee planted corn along rivers. They added beans and squash to their fields. Beans, corn, and squash were called the Three Sisters because the plants grew well together. The Cherokee also planted tobacco, pumpkins, and sunflowers. The Creek grew melon and sweet potatoes. The growing season was long, so fields were planted twice each year. The first planting was done in spring, with a second planting in midsummer.

Corn was often roasted or boiled. The people also made corn into flour or succotash, a dish of beans and corn. When the corn was harvested, the people celebrated with ceremonial dances. The Green Corn Ceremony, also called the Busk, is still celebrated in the Southeast.

A member of the Creek Nation wears a traditional deerskin vest.

## Clothing

When the weather was mild, Southeast Indians did not need much clothing. Men and boys wore breechcloths made of animal skin. Women and girls

# USING EVERY RESOURCE

Southeast Indians tried to use every part of the animals they hunted. Animal skins, bones, furs, and feathers were made into clothing, weapons, and shelters. The Timucua made hoes from fish bones attached to wood handles. The Catawba turned gourds into bowls, spoons, and cups. Stones, shells, and bones were used as fishing tools.

**Cherokee stone tools and a deer antler knife**

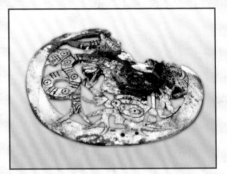

**A carved shell made for chiefs to wear**

wore wraparound skirts. Natchez women made their skirts from the inner bark of mulberry trees. Chickasaw women made theirs from deerskin. In cooler weather, they wore warm shawls made of soft animal skin. They added leggings, capes, and moccasins. Tunica men and women wore cloaks of mulberry cloth, woven turkey feathers, or muskrat fur during the cold seasons.

By the age of three, boys dressed like their fathers and uncles. Boys wore knee-length shirts with a belt made of

A Seminole mother stands with her children in Florida around 1917.

leather, yarn, or beads. Older girls dressed like their mothers and aunts. They wore long skirts and blouses. As girls grew older, they wore strings of beads around their necks and three long skirts at once.

# CHAPTER 2

# COMMUNITY AND
# SPIRITUALITY

**M**embers of a Southeast Indian village helped one another. Chiefs gave extra food to needy families. People from nearby villages sometimes joined together to fight a common enemy. Families traveled long distances to join in ceremonial dances and feasts. During gatherings, chiefs made important decisions, settled arguments, or planned for war.

Southeast Indians belonged to family-based groups called clans. These large groups of people share a common ancestor. People in the same clan could be close or distant relatives who lived in different communities. Men from the same clan often went on trading and hunting trips together. Women of a clan raised the children, cared for homes, and tended crops in fields and gardens.

## Leadership

Each Southeast Indian nation had its own government. In some nations, leaders were born into their roles. In others, such as the Cherokee, leaders were chosen by village members. The Creek and the Cherokee had both peace chiefs and war chiefs. The peace chiefs were also known as white chiefs. They governed the village in times of peace. The war chiefs were also known as red chiefs. A red chief was in charge of military matters.

Most Southeast Indian chiefs did not rule alone. They had a council to help them. The Cherokee village council was made up of nine men. They met in the main council house and made important decisions for the village.

## Roles of Men and Women

Women played important roles in Southeast societies. They were mothers, builders, healers, warriors, farmers, and craftswomen. In most groups, women were the heads of the households.

While most Southeast Indian chiefs were men, women played other important leadership roles. Cherokee council meetings were open to men and women. Cherokee "war women" were

This is a replica of a traditional Cherokee council house, a common site for Cherokee meetings.

**Portrait of Seminole Indian children and a Seminole Indian adult**

**M**ost Southeast Indian children worked alongside older family members from a young age. Girls helped sew and learned to make soup and bread. Women also taught girls to make baskets, pottery, and clothing. Girls helped their mothers and aunts care for younger children and older family members too. As they grew older, girls had jobs such as growing, preserving, and storing food.

Boys fished and gathered wood for fires. As they grew older, they learned to build homes, make weapons, clear land for farming, and fight in case their nation went to war.

respected and honored for their bravery. They were chosen by the red chief to go to war with the Cherokee men. Cherokee women also owned the family house and all the buildings.

Yet women were not considered equal in all Southeast Indian cultures. Natchez men were leaders of their communities. They were in charge of the household and ate their meals first. Natchez women farmed, gathered wild plants to eat, cooked, and preserved food. They made household goods such as clothing and baskets. Women also handled the early education of children.

## Beliefs

Southeast Indians believe that every creature has a spirit. Animal spirits share the world with the spirits of plants, rocks, the sun, and people who have died. Southeast Indians pray to the spirits through music, dance, ceremonies, and medicine rituals.

For many Southeast peoples, the sun was the highest power. The ancient Mound Builders kept a flame burning in the center of their towns as a symbol of the sun. The leader of the Natchez Nation was called the Great Sun. The Yuchi call themselves children of the sun, and the Creek worshipped the sun as the Great Spirit.

## Rituals

Southeast Indians performed rituals to ensure a good hunt, victory in battle, or a successful new year. The Cherokee celebrated their new year in fall, with the Great New Moon Festival. Because the number seven was sacred to the Cherokee, the men hunted for seven days before the festival. Seven women prepared the food.

For most Southeast peoples, corn harvesttime is the beginning of the New Year. The Green Corn Ceremony is the most important festival for groups such as the Creek, Cherokee, Seminole, and Yuchi. In June or

Many Southeast Indians consider corn harvesttime the beginning of the New Year.

July, the people give thanks for the first ripe corn of the season by gathering to dance, sing, and tell stories.

## Medicine

Southeast Indians also used ceremonies for healing the sick or hurt. For the Chickasaw and Choctaw, the *pashofa* dance was an important ritual for healing. In this ritual, a healer prayed while the family of the sick person gathered outside to dance, pray, and sing. Guests were served a corn soup called pashofa, which was cooked in the yard in a large pot.

Southeast Indians gathered wild plants to use in traditional medicine. The Catawba picked holly leaves and a plant called stinging nettle for medicinal tea. The Cherokee used roots from butternut trees to treat tooth pain. Each healer carried a small bundle that held roots, herbs, bones, and feathers. Medicine bundles were sacred, and their contents were usually secret.

Many Southeast peoples used the root of the butternut tree for medicine and the wood for carving.

Healers of most nations, including the Cherokee, Seminole, and Catawba, led sweat lodge ceremonies. This ceremony is still practiced. The lodge is a dome-shaped hut made with bent branches. River

Southeast peoples often use fires in traditional ceremonies.

rocks are tossed on a fire in the lodge, and water is poured over them to make steam. People then sit in the lodge and participate in ceremonial prayer. They sweat to remove disease from the body and the spirit.

# CHAPTER 3

# ART, MUSIC, AND DANCE

**S**outheast Indians are skilled craftspeople. Traditionally, they made baskets, pots, dolls, jewelry, and decorative clothing. They dyed and painted baskets and pots with color from roots, stones, mushrooms, nuts, and berries. They collected their materials from the rivers, hills, and forests around them. Many Southeast peoples still make craft items in traditional ways.

## Pottery and Baskets

Members of the Caddo Nation made decorated pots and bottles in many different styles. The Cherokee and other women made clay pots and containers for flowers, spices, and food. The Catawba used clay from what is now called the Catawba River. Most potters baked their clay creations over a fire to dry and harden. The Calusa hardened their clay in sand.

Southeast peoples are known for their baskets. Baskets were used to gather crops and store food. Only the women made baskets. Cherokee women used white oak and river cane for their baskets. The Seminole used sweetgrass, which has a long-lasting fragrance. Many Southeast women, including the

# SOUTHEAST INDIAN ART FORMS

| PEOPLE | ART FORMS |
|--------|-----------|
| Calusa | Pottery |
| Catawba | Pottery |
| Cherokee | Baskets, masks, painted flutes, and rattles |
| Chickasaw | Wooden figures |
| Chitimacha | Baskets |
| Seminole | Patchwork quilts, flutes, and dolls |

A Chitimacha basket

Seminole dolls

Cherokee and Seminole, also made baskets from bundled pine needles. They dyed the baskets with the juice of berries, nuts, and roots.

Basket designs were handed down from mother to daughter. Basket colors and design often represented the clan membership of the woman who made the basket. Some Chitimacha (CHEET-uh-muh-chah) women made baskets shaped like hearts. Women from other Chitimacha families used patterns that looked like the rattlesnakes or trout found in the area.

## Fabric Art

Many Southeast Indians made art from fabric they had traded from the Europeans. Seminole women cut long strips of calico fabric and dyed them. They used red, blue, or black fabric, sewn together into patchwork. They used the multicolored patchwork for their skirts and for men's shirts. Seminole women added embroidery. Catawba and Cherokee women sewed strips of ribbon onto their skirts. They also made colorful shawls from sheep's wool.

## Jewelry

The Cherokee made jewelry of shells and silver. Choctaw women's haircombs were made of silver or copper. They also painted clay beads to use in jewelry. Some Choctaw bead designs looked like sunbursts. Other designs were shaped like human figures. The Seminole made rings and bracelets of silver. Women often sewed silver jewelry onto their patchwork

## TOYS AND DOLLS

Southeast Indians made toys using materials they found around them. Boys were given small bows and arrows to learn hunting skills. Girls were given dolls, often with tiny cradleboards, which are boards used to carry infants on the back. Chickasaw women made beaded dolls. Women sewed clothing for the dolls that matched their own bright skirts and capes. Some traditional Seminole dolls are only 3 inches (7.6 centimeters) tall.

These pieces of Seminole jewelry were found near Tampa Bay, Florida.

skirts. Seminole women wrapped many strings of beads around their necks. As women grew older, they wore more and more beaded necklaces.

## Carvings and Masks

Wood carving was a valued skill passed down by Southeast men. Caddo men carved wooden bowls, chests, chairs, beds, and arrows. These were made of woods such as cypress. The Cherokee men carved utensils and furniture from many types of trees, including walnut and cherry. They also carved pipes, beads, and jewelry from stone. Calusa men carved wooden turtles, alligators, and panthers.

Southeastern craftspeople also carved masks for dances. The Cherokee men carved painted masks that often had fur decorations. These were called booger masks after *bogey*, an

English word for "ghost." Warriors wore these masks before a battle. Wearing the masks, they danced and laughed to make fun of their enemies. After the arrival of the Europeans, the masks were carved with long noses, mustaches, and beards to look like Europeans. Cherokee men wore the masks in dances to scare away the spirit of the illnesses brought by Europeans.

## Dances

Southeast Indians held lively dances throughout the year. Many peoples, including the Cherokee, performed the eagle dance, which celebrated both peace and war. Dancers waved eagle feathers and wore them on their heads and backs as they performed.

Many ceremonies included stomp dancing. In this style of dance, men, women, and sometimes children formed a single line behind a healer. The dancers gently stomped their feet, sang, and moved in a weaving line for hours. They wore shells and rattles on their legs that clinked and shook. Some ceremonies still include stomp dancing.

Men and women wore ceremonial clothing for dances. Choctaw women wore flowing skirts with ruffled white aprons. Cherokee women wore turtle shell rattles on their knees during dances, and

The Cherokee made rattles from gourds for ceremonial songs.

Stomp dancing is still a common practice in ceremonies and festivals.

many men and women wore leg rattles made from shells, deer hooves, or bones. Chickasaw men often wore hair roaches. These headdresses ran down the middle of their shaved scalps.

Most of these dances are still performed at ceremonies. Some are private religious rituals. Others, like the Busk, are open to the public. Often the celebration includes competitive dances among groups from many regions.

# CHAPTER 4
# PEACETIME AND WARTIME

**W**hen Europeans began to arrive in the Southeast, they were looking for gold and land to claim for their countries. At first, the Southeast Indians traded with the Europeans. They exchanged animal meat, skins, and furs for European tools, beads, cloth, and weapons. But contact with Europeans soon brought death, disease, and displacement to the Southeast peoples.

A Southeast Indian family canoes to a coastal trading post.

## New Arrivals

One of the first Europeans to reach the Southeast was Spanish explorer Juan Ponce de León in 1513. He was sent by the king of Spain to find and to claim land for the Spanish. He and his crew landed near Saint Augustine in present-day Florida. He met small groups of Southeast Indians, including the Tequesta.

In 1521 Ponce de León arrived on a second trip to Florida. Word had traveled through the Southeast that the Spanish wanted to move onto Southeast lands to farm. This time, Ponce de León sailed into Calusa land off the Gulf of Florida. He brought more than two hundred Spaniards with him.

The Calusa were prepared to protect their homeland. Calusa in eighty canoes met the Spanish ships to try to keep them from landing. The Spanish attacked. The Calusa had bows and arrows for weapons, while the Spanish had firearms. The Spanish captured Calusa women and destroyed canoes. In the fighting, Ponce de León was shot and killed by a Calusa's arrow.

From 1539 to 1543, Spanish explorer Hernando de Soto traveled across the Southeast. His crew was on a quest to find gold and to claim land. De Soto and his men received gifts such as pearls and copper from the Southeast Indians. But de Soto and his army of seven hundred soldiers took slaves at every village. They planned to use the slaves as guides and laborers. They often burned villages to the ground to weaken the power of the Southeast Indians. Soon the Chickasaw, Timucua, and other groups saw that the Spanish planned to take over their homelands.

## Nations in Conflict

Some Europeans used Southeast Indians to fight other Europeans who hoped to live on Southeast Indian land. In the 1670s, the

English fought alongside the Creek against the Spanish.

During the American Revolution (1775-1783), British colonists in North America fought Great Britain for their independence. The Catawba helped the colonists, while the Cherokee fought on the side of the British. The Choctaw did not want to choose sides. They knew that when the war ended, there could be dangerous consequences.

The Cherokee paid for helping the British. In 1776, the year the colonists declared independence, the US Army attacked the Cherokee Nation. The Cherokee did not want to get into a direct battle with the better armed US forces. Many Cherokee fled west. The soldiers destroyed the homes and crops they left behind.

## Missions

The Spanish government directed explorers to bring Christianity to the Southeast Indians. Many Spanish people used their religion as a tool to control the Southeast Indians. In 1565 the Spanish built a mission in modern-day Florida. The missionaries taught the Southeast Indians the ways of Europeans. They instructed them in Christianity, farming, and ranching. By 1740 there were more than sixty missions in present-day Florida alone.

Some Southeast Indians fought their own wars against the Europeans and the United States. By 1790 about one million Europeans had come to the Southeast. The Southeast Indians knew that the colonists were not leaving. Some Southeast Indians, including the Cherokee, began to adopt European customs and lifestyles. Europeans hoped the Southeast Indians would give up their land and traditions. The European newcomers called the Cherokee, Chickasaw, Choctaw, Creek, and Seminole the Five

Civilized Nations. The Europeans believed these peoples were more like Europeans than other Southeast peoples.

## Death and Disease

Wherever Europeans traveled, they carried germs. These germs were new to the Southeast peoples. They had no immunity to fight diseases such as cholera and smallpox. The diseases spread through the Southeast, killing tens of thousands. By the early 1800s, about 80 percent of the American Indians in present-day Florida had died. By 1826 only 110 people remained in the Catawba Nation.

With their populations shrinking, the Southeast Indians

# OSCEOLA

**Seminole warrior Osceola**

Osceola (ah-see-OH-luh) was a Seminole warrior who was born in Alabama. He rejected US government treaties that would force his people to move to Oklahoma. In 1837 Osceola was invited to meet members of the US Army for peace talks. The Seminole wanted peace, and they went to meet the army at Saint Augustine with a white flag that signaled their desire for peace. US soldiers then captured Osceola and sent him to prison in South Carolina. He died there in 1838.

# THE SEMINOLE WARS

In the nineteenth century, the Seminole waged several wars against US troops to try to protect their homeland. The First Seminole War (1817–1818) was fought against General Andrew Jackson, who later became president of the United States. Jackson and his army were sent to defend Europeans who'd moved to Seminole land. The Seminole won that war, but their villages were burned.

The Second Seminole War (1835–1842) began near present-day Tampa, Florida. When a Seminole group was attacked by US soldiers, the Seminole warriors killed all but 3 of them. Four days later, 250 Seminole warriors attacked 750 US soldiers. Again, the Seminole defeated them, winning the war.

The Third Seminole War (1855–1858) began when the Seminole launched attacks against white traders and trappers. The US Army once again tried to defeat the Seminole but failed. The Seminole remained in their homeland. Over time, however, many Europeans moved to the land as well. Many Seminole still live in Florida.

knew they could not defend themselves and their land alone. They hoped they would be stronger if they joined together. The Natchez and Yuchi, for example, joined the Creek Confederacy.

## Resistance and Removal

In 1830 US president Andrew Jackson signed the Indian Removal Act. This allowed the government to set aside lands west of the Mississippi River, in present-day Oklahoma, for American Indians. The government called the land Indian Territory.

By 1831 few Southeast Indian groups had volunteered to leave their homeland for Indian Territory. The US government decided to remove them by force. Between 1831 and 1839, many of the Choctaw, Seminole, Creek, Chickasaw, Cherokee, and others were forced to leave their lands.

US soldiers forced Southeast Indians to walk or ride on wagons and boats for nearly 1,000 miles (1,609 kilometers). There was not enough food, blankets, or clothing. More than four thousand Cherokee died from cold, hunger, and illness. The forced march became known as the Trail of Tears.

Once in Indian Territory, the Southeast Indians tried to create a stable life for themselves. The men focused on clearing areas for farms. The land was different from what they had known in the Southeast, and in many places, the soil was not as rich.

The Trail of Tears refers to many routes taken during the forced removal of Southeast peoples to reservations.

# SEQUOYAH

**S**equoyah (seh-KOY-uh) was a Cherokee born around 1776 in what is now the state of Tennessee. He designed an alphabet for his people. It consists of eighty-six characters, or graphic symbols used to make words. Sequoyah's alphabet allowed the Cherokee to write in their own language. The Cherokee were then able to write books, newspapers, and other materials. The Cherokee still use Sequoyah's alphabet.

The women tended the fields and made pottery, baskets, and clothing. They raised their children in the unfamiliar landscape of the Midwest.

Lands that were set aside as territory for American Indians became known as reservations. The US government controlled many aspects of life on the reservations. It even had the right to choose council members and chiefs. Still, the nations governed themselves the best they could. The Cherokee Nation wrote their first constitution in 1839.

Not all Southeast Indians were removed from their lands. Many of the Cherokee that remained in the Southeast became US citizens. Other small groups of Cherokee and Choctaw hid from European Americans in woodlands. The Cherokee that

This 1942 painting shows the Trail of Tears.

were forced to move to Indian Territory became known as the Western Cherokee, while those that remained became the Eastern Cherokee. A few smaller groups, including the Catawba in present-day South Carolina and the Monacan in present-day Virginia, also remained in the Southeast.

# CHAPTER 5

# BLENDING PAST AND FUTURE

**I**n 1924 American Indians became US citizens **under the Indian Citizenship Act.** Individual states still decided whether American Indians could vote in US elections. In 1957 all American Indians were given the right to vote. In the 1970s, American Indians won the legal freedom to govern themselves.

In the 1960s, the American Indian Movement (AIM) was created. People from nations across the United States protested unfair treatment of American Indians. AIM worked to help American Indian nations reclaim lands that had been taken from them by the US government.

In the 1990s, nations from the Southeast continued to work with the US government to reclaim their homelands. The government offered money to some nations in exchange for their land. Some nations, such as the Seminole, refused the money. Other nations accepted money and used it to better their communities. Some were able to reclaim the homelands of their ancestors. In 2006 the sacred mound of Nanih Waiya in Mississippi was returned to the Choctaw.

## Today

Many Southeast Indians make their living by farming. They grow lemons, grapefruit, and oranges to sell in markets across the country. Others work in construction. Chickasaw and Choctaw firms provide construction and technology services. The Seminole and others work in tourism, giving people tours of Southeast lands and building casinos. Many Southeast Indians have started their own businesses and sell their arts and crafts.

## Caring for the Land

Southeast Indians care for their lands for future generations. Most of the Florida Seminole lands lie in the swamps of the Everglades, sometimes called the River of Grass. Many endangered animals and plants live there, including the last of the Florida panthers. The Seminole people have created many programs to keep the land healthy. They teach tourists and others about the importance of the Everglades in nature and in their culture.

Members of the Eastern Band of Cherokee work with the Tree Improvement Program at the University of Tennessee. This program works to save butternut trees, many of which have been

A Seminole woman makes traditional baskets at a festival in Florida.

killed by disease. The Cherokee use the butternut wood for carving. Traditionally, they ate the tree's nuts and used the roots for medicine. Cherokee women still use the butternut tree for basketmaking. They make dyes from the nuts and bark.

## Keeping Traditions Alive

Many nations hold public celebrations and dances year-round. They share traditional arts, crafts, and music. Storytellers share many stories passed down from their ancestors. The Miccosukee (mick-o-SOO-kee) Indian Arts and Crafts Festival brings American Indian artists from across North America to Florida every year. They sell their crafts, textiles, and pottery. Many nations, including the Seminole, run villages and museums where visitors can learn about the history and culture of Southeast Indians.

American Indians of the Southeast are a large, diverse group of cultures with many similarities and differences among them. They share a desire to honor the land, their traditions, and their culture. Southeast Indian nations continue to live

# CHEROKEE NATIONAL HOLIDAY

The Cherokee Nation Constitution was signed in 1839. This organized the Cherokee Nation under one government. Every year the nation hosts a three-day celebration of Cherokee heritage in Tahlequah, Oklahoma. Visitors play traditional American Indian games such as marbles and stickball.

The traditional game of stickball is similar to lacrosse and is popular among many Southeast nations and other nations.

according to these values so their traditions can be passed on to new generations.

The Cherokee hold an annual event called Remember the Removal Bike Ride. Teams meet in Georgia and bike 950 miles (1,529 km). The ride takes three weeks. The route follows the path their ancestors traveled when they were forced from the Southeast. It is a powerful reminder of the journey of the American Indians and their efforts to remember their ancestors and their homeland.

### Diane Glancy (Cherokee)

is a novelist, poet, and playwright. Her book characters often express how removal must have felt to the Southeast Indians: "They couldn't remove us. Didn't the soldiers know we were the land? The cornstalks were our grandmothers. . . . Their voices were the long tassels reaching the air. Our spirits clung to them. Our roots entwined." She has won many awards for her writing, including the American Book Award for her book *Claiming Breath* in 1993.

### Bobby Frank (Seminole)

is a traditional arts teacher. At the Culture Department of the Seminole Nation in Florida, he and his coworkers teach the arts of Seminole patchwork, basketry, and wood carving to children. He says, "We want to get younger people interested in traditional crafts. We don't want these old designs to be lost." He teaches children to make traditional designs, including the crawfish, rain, fire, and man-on-horse patterns.

### John Herrington (Chickasaw)

is an astronaut. He was the flight engineer aboard the space shuttle *Endeavour* in 2002. During that flight, he became the first American Indian to go on a space walk. Herrington honored his Chickasaw heritage by carrying six eagle feathers, a braid of sweetgrass, two arrowheads, and the flag of the Chickasaw Nation.

### Yona FrenchHawk (North Carolina Cherokee)

is a ceremonial singer. In addition to singing, he chants, drums, and waves eagle feathers when performing ceremonies. The Cherokee have traditionally used eagle feathers to call on the bird's spirit. FrenchHawk says, "We believe when you have an eagle feather, you will always find your way home. To my people, home is the place where the fire burns within."

# Timeline

Each Southeast Indian culture had its own way of recording history. This timeline is based on the Gregorian calendar, which Europeans brought to North America.

**800 CE**   Corn is introduced to the Southeast. Permanent settlements become common as Southeast Indians settle on farmland.

**1541–1543**   Spaniard Hernando de Soto arrives in South Florida and meets the Cherokee, Creek, and Calusa.

**1817–1818**   The first Seminole War is fought between the US government and the Seminole people.

**1830**   President Andrew Jackson signs the Indian Removal Act.

**1831–1839**   Most Creek, Choctaw, Chickasaw, Cherokee, and Seminole are removed to reservations in Oklahoma Indian Territory.

**1835–1842**   The Second Seminole War is fought.

**1855–1858**   The Third Seminole war is fought.

**1924**   The Indian Citizenship Act allows all American Indians to become US citizens.

**1934**   The opening of Great Smoky Mountains National Park brings tourists to the Eastern Band of Cherokee's homeland.

**1985**   Wilma Mankiller is the first woman elected chief of the Western Cherokee Nation.

**1988**   The Trail of Tears is named a US National Historic Landmark.

**1989**   A Tequesta village is uncovered in downtown Miami, Florida.

**2006**   Nanih Waiya in Mississippi is returned to the Choctaw.

**2013**   The Cherokee Nation holds the first Cherokee Nation Environmental Festival near Tahlequah, Oklahoma, on April 13.

# Glossary

**breechcloth:** an apron-like garment that was often made of animal skin

**ceremony:** a spiritual celebration or event

**confederacy:** two or more nations that join together

**council:** a group of people that come together to make decisions

**cradleboard:** a board used to carry infants on the back

**dugout canoe:** a canoe made from a hollowed-out tree trunk

**elder:** an older American Indian who passes on knowledge and traditions

**headdress:** a ceremonial head decoration that sometimes includes bird feathers

**language family:** a group of similar languages

**mission:** a group of people doing religious work or the building in which they work

**nation:** an independent group of people with a shared history, culture, and governing system

**peoples:** nations or groups of related nations

**reservation:** an area of land set aside by the US government for the use of an American Indian nation

**ritual:** a religious or spiritual ceremony

**treaty:** a formal agreement between two or more nations or peoples

## Source Notes

42  Bobby Frank, phone interview with the author, February 2, 2015.

42  Yona FrenchHawk, phone interview with the author, January 24, 2015.

42  Diane Glancy, *Pushing the Bear*. New York: Harcourt, 1996, 4.

## Selected Bibliography

Pauketat, Timothy, and Nancy Stone Bernard. *Cahokia Mounds*. New York: Oxford University Press, 2004.

Rozema, Vicki. *Footsteps of the Cherokees*. Winston-Salem, NC: John F. Blair, 2007.

Treuer, A. *Indian Nations of North America*. Washington DC: National Geographic, 2013.

LERNER

SOURCE™

Expand learning beyond the printed book. Download free, complementary educational resources for this book from our website, www.lerneresource.com.

## Further Information

Carlson, Lori Marie, ed. *Moccasin Thunder: American Indian Stories for Today*. New York: HarperCollins, 2005. Read short stories by American Indian writers about the lives of teenagers on and off reservations.

Josephson, Judith Pinkerton. *Why Did Cherokees Move West? And Other Questions about the Trail of Tears*. Minneapolis: Lerner Publications, 2011. Read more about how thirteen thousand Cherokee were forced on the 1,000-mile (1,609 km) journey to Oklahoma.

Sanford, William R.. *Seminole Chief Osceola*. Berkeley Heights, NJ: Enslow, 2013. Discover more about the life of Chief Osceola and his war to save the lands of the Seminole people.

The Seminole Tribe of Florida
http://www.semtribe.com
Visit the offical website of the Seminole tribe of Florida to read about their history, culture, government, and more.

Smith, Cynthia Leitich. *Indian Shoes*. New York: HarperCollins, 2002. This collection of stories follows Ray, a Seminole-Cherokee boy living with his grandfather in Chicago, Illinois.

Sonneborn, Liz. *Wilma Mankiller*. New York: Marshall Cavendish, 2011. Learn more about the life of Wilma Mankiller, the first woman elected to lead the Cherokee Nation.

Tieck, Sarah. *Seminole*. Minneapolis: Big Buddy Books, 2015. Read more about how the Seminole traditionally lived, from their homes and food to the importance of storytelling in the Seminole culture.

## Index

American Indian Movement (AIM), 38

American Revolution, 32

Appalachian Mountains, 8, 10, 12

Atlantic Ocean, 10, 12

ceremonies, 12, 15, 18, 21–23, 28–29

clans, 18, 25

clothing, 10, 15–17, 20, 24, 26, 28, 35–36

crafts, 19, 24–27, 39, 40

Creek Confederacy, 7, 34

dance, 12, 15, 18, 21–22, 27, 28–29, 40

food, 10, 14–15, 18, 20, 21, 24, 35

Green Corn Ceremony (Busk), 15, 21, 29

Gulf of Mexico, 10

health, 9, 22–23, 30, 33

housing, 11–13

Indian Citizenship Act, 38

Indian Removal Act, 34

Indian Territory, 35, 37

isolate languages, 7

Jackson, Andrew, 34

jewelry, 24, 26–27

leadership, 18–21

missions, 32

Mississippi River, 6, 34

modern life, 39–41

Osceola, 33

Remember the Removal Bike Ride, 41

reservations, 36

Seminole Wars, 34

Sequoyah, 36

spirituality, 21, 28

trade, 10, 18, 26, 30, 34

Trail of Tears, 35

Tree Improvement Program, 40

## Photo Acknowledgments

The images in this book are used with the permission of: © iStockphoto.com/Bastar (paper background); © lienkie/123RF.com (tanned hide background); © Minden Pictures RM/Getty Images, pp. 2–3; © Laura Westlund/Independent Picture Service, pp. 4, 6, 35; © Ditch Fisher/Wikimedia Commons (CC BY-SA 3.0), p. 7; The Granger Collection, New York, pp. 11, 37; © Marilyn Angel Wynn/Nativestock.com, pp. 12, 15, 16 (both), 19, 25 (bottom), 27, 28, 29, 39, 41; © North Wind Picture Archives, p. 13; © Corbis, p. 17; Courtesy of the State Archives of Florida, p. 20; © Stephen Shepherd/Photolibrary RM/Getty Images, p. 21; © Scimat Scimat/Photo Researchers RM/Getty Images, p. 22; © Peter Walton Photography/Photolibrary RM/Getty Images, p. 23; © CPC Collection/Alamy, p. 25 (top); © History Miami, Florida, USA/A. Kaufmann/Bridgeman Images, p. 30; © Catlin, George/Bridgeman Images, p. 33; © Everett Collection Inc/Alamy, p. 36; © Chris Felver/Getty Images, p. 42 (top); © Brian Clearly/AFP/Getty Images, p. 42 (bottom).

Front cover: © iStockphoto.com/Warren Price.